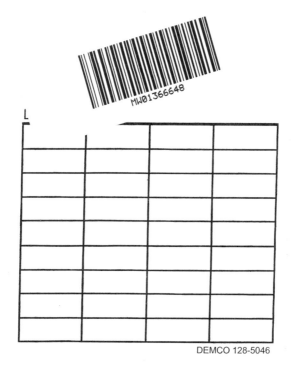

Outcast and Hero

The Setbacks and Comebacks of
Mildred "Babe" Didrikson Zaharias

Cos Ferrara

Mildred "Babe" Didrikson Zaharias

Outcast and Hero, The Setbacks and Comebacks of Mildred "Babe" Didrikson Zaharias, Copyright, © 2004 by Girls Explore™ LLC

All rights reserved. No part of this book may be used or reproduced in any manner whatsoever without written permission of the publisher except in the case of brief quotations embodied in critical articles and reviews. For information address Girls Explore™ LLC, P.O. Box 54, Basking Ridge, NJ 07920, www.girls-explore.com.

Library of Congress Control Number: 2004109361

ISBN 0-9749456-2-5

Printed in the United States of America
10 9 8 7 6 5 4 3 2 1

Photo Credits:

Courtesy of the Babe Didrikson Zaharias Foundation, pp. 11, 98; Courtesy of AP/WIDE WORLD PHOTOS, pp. 34, 73, 81, 86, 90, 92, 94; Courtesy of the Tyrrell Historical Library, p. 17, Lamar University, Mary and John Gray Library Archives and Special Collections, pp.8, 12, 20, 21, 26, 52, 68, 71, 75, 97, Courtesy of Bettmann/CORBIS, pp. 31, 41, 42, 45, 50, 56, 60, 63, 66, 84, 85, 100

Cover Illustration Courtesy of Bettman/Corbis

Cover Design - Chris Kelley – Jon Reis Photo + Design
Interior Design – Vernon Thornblad PoGo Studio

from WHATTA-GIRL by William Oscar Johnson and Nancy Williamson
Copyright (c) 1977 by William Oscar Johnson and Nancy Williamson
Published by Little Brown & Co., New York
Used by permission of the Wallace Literary Agency, Inc

Contents

    Introduction 4
1 Growing Up Poor But Happy 9
2 Outcast and Hero 19
3 Babe Makes Her Move 24
4 Olympic Hero 36
5 Babe's Fall from Grace 47
6 Babe Climbs Back to the Top 54
7 Babe Marries George Zaharias 70
8 Babe Hits Her Stride 78
9 Woman of the Year 88
10 Babe Faces Up to Her Final Challenge . . 96

    Babe's Record of Achievement 102
    Visit the Babe Didrikson Zaharias Museum
    References 103
    Endnotes 104

Introduction

How would you feel if your teammates laughed at you behind your back? Or if people tried to keep you from doing what you loved because your family was poor? Would you quit the team? Would you stop doing what you loved? That's not what Babe Didrikson Zaharias did. The more they laughed, the harder she worked. The more barriers people put up, the more determined she became to knock them down.

Mildred "Babe" Didrikson Zaharias played just about everything. And she was good at whatever she played. She won All America honors in basketball. She played baseball, tennis, and volleyball. She single-handedly scored 30 points in an AAU (Amateur Athletic Union) track and field meet when her closest rival—an entire team of 20 athletes—scored only 22 points. She won two Olympic gold medals for track and field. She dominated women's golf for years and founded the Ladies Professional Golf Association. She was chosen Woman Athlete of the Year six different times over a period of 20 years. In 1949, she was named Woman Athlete of the First Half of the 20th century. And she was named Woman of the Year, an honor that goes beyond the world of sports. Looking back on the 20th Century, ESPN ranked her the number 10 athlete, the top woman. With all of these acknowledgements, you might think Babe's life was full of nothing but joy. That's not true at all.

For much of her life, Babe was a victim—a victim of prejudice. When she was in school, the other girls would compliment her for playing a great basketball game. Then those same girls would talk about Babe behind her back. They would make fun of the way she dressed and cut her hair. Babe didn't like the frilly styles of clothes that most girls wore. She didn't want to fuss to make her hair long and soft and wavy. Like other victims of prejudice, Babe was made an outcast because she was different.

People even criticized the way she played basketball. Teammates and others were happy when Babe led the team to one championship after another. But then they said Babe played the game more like the boys—crashing into people and muscling her way to the basket.

The boys treated Babe much the way the girls did. They admired her athletic skills but not the girl herself. For one thing, many realized she was a better athlete than they were. So they felt intimidated. For another, Babe was not "feminine" enough for them. It was OK to cheer her from the stands when she played for the school team. But asking this "manly" girl out on a date was out of the question.

Later in life, when Babe became a golf champion, she felt the prejudice of wealthy people from the country club set. They didn't think it proper that this poor girl was so successful at golf. Until that time, golf was a sport played only by the wealthy. "We don't want a truck driver's daughter playing here," was the way one club member put it.

Babe was also the victim of gender prejudice. Many people just did not like a girl or woman playing sports that boys and men played. Just as other women had to break down barriers to get into certain schools or professions, Babe had to break down barriers to be the athlete she wanted to be.

Through it all, Babe endured the ridicule and the taunting. She overlooked the snide remarks and the attempts to "keep her out." No matter how hard they tried to deprive Babe of the chance to succeed, she worked harder to overcome their prejudice. She let her actions do her talking, mostly. She reached a level in sports that no woman had even come close to before. She demonstrated such skill and determination that her critics either came over to her side or just stopped trying to hold her down.

Today hundreds of thousands of girls across America and the world play sports that once were limited to the

Introduction

boys. One of the key people who made that possible is Babe. Today, many women earn thousands—even millions—of dollars playing professional golf. They have Babe to thank because she started the Ladies Professional Golf Association.

As you read the life of Mildred "Babe" Didrikson Zaharias, you may not approve of some of Babe's behavior. For instance, she often boasted about her abilities. She'd taunt her competitors—as well as her teammates—when she'd say things like: "I don't know why you are practicing so hard just to come in second."[1] The others would get even angrier when Babe backed up her boast with the win. For another thing, she constantly sought attention and was always promoting herself to the press.

But you will also see much to admire. You'll see a girl/woman of great inner strength. You'll see a person who had the courage to withstand the critics and follow her dream. You'll see a woman who paved the way for other women to build successful careers playing professional golf. You'll see a woman whose fight against cancer brought hope and encouragement to others suffering from the disease.

In the end, the world recognized this brash woman from a poor immigrant family as not only a great athlete; they also saw her as a great American. They saw in Babe the rags-to-riches story. To them she embodied the American dream, rising from poverty to wealth, from outcast to hero.

Mildred "Babe" Didrikson Zaharias

Mildred "Babe" Didrikson Zaharias

1
Growing Up Poor But Happy

Mildred Ella "Babe" Didrikson Zaharias lived the American dream. She was the daughter of immigrant parents who came to America to make a better life for their children. "America is the land of opportunity," these new Americans had been told. "In America, dreams come true." Babe dreamed a dream and, because of her hard work, it came true. She rose from a humble birth to become one of the greatest athletes of all time. Fifty years after her death, Dave Anderson wrote in *The New York Times* that Babe "still ranks as this planet's most accomplished female athlete."[1]

Babe's parents came from their native Norway to settle in America in the early twentieth century. Babe's father Ole (O-Lay) came first. He took a job as a cabinetmaker and saved some money. Then he sent for his wife, Hannah, and their three children—Dora, Esther, and Nancy. Babe had not been born yet.

The family lived in Port Arthur, Texas. This was an oil-producing area near the Gulf of Mexico. Hannah didn't like the change. In Norway, she loved to ski and ice skate. (Babe may have inherited some of her athletic ability from her mother.) Hannah remembered the air in her homeland as being crisp and cool and clean. She found Port Arthur to be hot and humid. The residue from the oil refineries coated the streets and houses with a slick and smelly oil film.[2] Hannah also didn't like the constant noise in Port Arthur—the clatter of horse hoofs, the steam whistles from the docks, the clanging boxcars of the trains.[3]

Not long after the family settled into Port Arthur, twins Lillie and Louis were born. Then in 1911, Mildred (Babe) arrived. Like many immigrant families, the Didriksons used two languages. As they struggled to learn English in the outside world, they used the language of their ancestors inside the home. Sometimes they mixed the two. It was from this intertwining of languages that Mildred became "Babe." In her "broken" English, Hannah began calling her newborn "Mine Babe." Eventually, everyone called her "Babe." Later in life, Babe often said that she received the nickname because as a youngster she could hit a baseball as well as Babe Ruth. But that was just one of the "stories"[4] she told to entertain the press.

One day fierce winds uprooted homes in Port Arthur. Some 275 people died. Amidst this violent act of nature, Babe's younger brother was born. Because of the weather when he was born, the family named him Arthur Storm Didrikson. Giving the boy the middle name of "Storm" shows something about the family that influenced Babe. Though the Didriksons faced some very difficult struggles, they always managed to keep a sense of humor and keep plugging away. Babe showed the same kind of grit throughout her life in facing the tough times that came her way.

The Didrikson house was sturdy and withstood the hurricane winds. But rainwater sloshed through the house. All of the family's possessions were ruined. The family took what little they had left and moved to Beaumont, Texas, 17 miles away.[5]

The chief industry in Beaumont was oil. Hannah had

Babe's first photo

to endure the same smells and sounds and pollution as in Port Arthur. In addition, trolley tracks lined the street in

Babe with older sister Lillie and younger brother Arthur

front of the Didrikson's rented house on Doucette Street. So Hannah also heard the rumble of the trolley that ran back and forth outside her home.[6]

But Beaumont was different in some ways from Port Arthur. The town had its own radio station, a hotel, and restaurants. It also had a yacht club, a literary society, and a golf club. And it had some families that were fairly wealthy—rich, by some standards.[7]

The Didriksons were not wealthy. In fact, they were poor. Ole was a cabinet maker by trade. But that work was not steady. He often found himself out of work and out of money. Sometimes he signed on with an oil tanker and went off to sea for weeks at a time to earn money for his family. To help make ends meet, Hannah took in wash. She spent hours scrubbing by hand other people's dirty laundry. She wasn't paid much, but every little bit helped.[8]

Children often pitched in to raise money for family groceries, rent, and other needs. Babe sometimes helped her mother washing the clothes. Another of Babe's jobs was to brush a woman's hair for 10 cents. At age 12, Babe worked in a fig plant inspecting the fruit. When she found any figs with bad spots on them, she took those out of the batch. She peeled or cleaned away the spots and tossed the figs back into the trough. For this work Babe was paid 30 cents an hour. This job made Babe's hand so sore, she was having trouble holding and throwing a baseball. So she left that job when she found another in a gunnysack company. Gunnysack is coarse material used for making bags and rope. Babe's job involved taking a large piece of this material and sewing it into a bag. She was paid one cent for each bag she sewed. All but a nickel of Babe's pay each week went to the family.[9]

The children also helped out around the house. Babe and her sisters would often fight over who was to scrub the porch floor. When it was Babe's turn, she would tie brushes to her feet and "skate" around the porch until she had covered it with soap. Then she would rinse the brushes and skate over the porch again.[10]

Despite living in poverty, the family was loving and happy. "I had a wonderful childhood," Babe later wrote in her autobiography. "That must prove it doesn't take money to be happy, because the Didriksons weren't rich. My father and mother had to work and scrimp and save like anything just to be able to feed and clothe us all."[11]

Without much money, the Didriksons often found ways to entertain themselves. Music was a big part of their life. Esther and Dora played the piano. Ole played the violin. The brothers played drums. Hannah sang. And Babe played the harmonica.[12]

Another form of entertainment was storytelling. Ole would often delight his family with stories of his voyages at sea. He was very imaginative and would embellish an ordinary occurrence with creative details. He made the stories fun and exciting for the whole family. Ole's storytelling ability may have rubbed off on Babe, as we'll see later.

Ole also built a "gym" for the children to play on and strengthen themselves. He set up bars in the backyard for jumping. He used a broomstick and flatirons to make weights. This "equipment" was intended for the boys in the family but Babe and her sisters also used them.[13]

Though Babe was happy, she learned early on how hard life could be. She saw that her family was not alone in this struggle. Most families in her neighborhood lived the same way. Many poor women did menial jobs like scrubbing other people's wash and sewing gunnysacks. Watching her parents and neighbors struggle as they did, Babe was determined that her life would be different. She would develop her skills so she would not have to scrub other people's laundry or clean their homes to make a living.

Most of the kids living in the area of Beaumont where the Didriksons lived were poor and tough. They had very little and would not let anyone take away what little they had. That meant not only material things. It also included their sense of pride. Babe was very much like them. She was proud of who she was and of the family she came from. When others later tried to change her, Babe wouldn't surrender her own true self.

Babe was one of the most active kids on Doucette Street. Her brother said she always wanted to be running or jumping or throwing something.[14] One of Babe's favorite activities was racing the streetcar (trolley) as it rolled down Doucette Street.[15]

Without money to buy equipment or toys, these kids made up their own fun and games. They played pranks on the man who drove the trolley. Sometimes they played pranks on their teachers at school. One day Babe caused a stir at school. She climbed the flagpole and remained at the top until the school principal came out and ordered her down.[16]

Kids played circus by hanging from a sycamore tree in someone's yard. They played baseball with a taped-up ball and mitts they got with Octagon soap coupons. This kind of play was fun enough to keep Babe out all day. She went home only when she was hungry or when her parents called her.[17] Sometimes she'd totally forget about going home.

On the day Babe's sister Lillie was graduating from grammar school, Hannah sent Babe to the store for ground beef. Babe went to the store, bought the meat, and started home. But she saw a baseball game in progress. She went over and was soon playing. The meat sat on a bench in the warm sun. After some time, Lillie came looking for her. But by then, the beef had spoiled. Babe "heard about it" from her mother that day.[18]

Between Babe's house and the grocery store down the block there were seven homes. Each had a hedge running from the porch to the sidewalk. When Babe had to go to the store, she wouldn't walk or run on the sidewalk. She would run across the lawns, hurdling the hedges as she went. One hedge, however, was higher than the others. That threw off Babe's timing. So she went up to the owner of that house and explained the problem. She asked the owner if he would trim his hedges to the same height as the others. The owner did.[19]

In Magnolia Elementary School, Babe wasn't much interested in the things most young girls were interested in. At the time, most girls had to take sewing and cooking classes, as they were being trained to be homemakers.

Babe's entry in the 1929 Pine Burr, *her high school yearbook.*

MILDRED "BABE" DIDRIKSEN

Forward

"Babe," has been a very necessary player on the Miss Royal Purple squad this year. She never failed to star in any game, at home or abroad. She is a very capable forward, who very seldom misses the basket. When "Babe" gets the ball, the scorekeeper gets his adding machine, and then he sometimes loses count. B. H. S. will have her again next year.

Babe's entry in her high school yearbook shows her to be a star athlete at an early age.

Babe once made a dress in sewing class that won a prize at the Texas State Fair. She was proud of that dress. But she didn't care much for cooking class.[20]

Her personality was different from that of most girls. Girls in those days were supposed to be acting in ways that prepared them for their role as mothers. Babe was different. She'd give a hand when needed, but her competitive spirit drove her to always want to be first.[21] And while Babe enjoyed her home and family life very much, she loved sports.

Babe was blessed with a great deal of natural athletic ability. And forces around her also encouraged her in the direction of sports. One of those forces was her father. He followed the sports news in the papers, and he talked to the children about the different games and teams. That's how Babe began reading the sports pages when she was very young. "Before I was in even into my teens," Babe wrote in her autobiography, "I knew what I wanted to be when I grew up. My goal was to be the greatest athlete that ever lived."[22]

◆◆◆

2

Hero And Outcast

When Babe was a student at Magnolia Elementary, there were no teams for girls. But older girls often came to the school to play basketball. Babe pestered them to let her play. Finally they did. She quickly made a few baskets and the girls said, "If you were bigger and older we'd want you on our team."[1] Hearing that, Babe couldn't wait to enter junior high.

There was a girls basketball team in Beaumont's Davy Crockett Junior High and Babe was on it. She played well and developed her game. But when she got to high school, the coach told her she was too small. (Even when she won the gold at the Olympics, Babe was not much taller than five feet and weighed only 105 pounds. So she was even smaller in her early high school years.) But Babe was determined to show that, despite her lack of height, she could play basketball. She might be shorter, but she would prove to be better. She went to the coach of the boys' team. She said: "Coach Dimmit, will you teach me to play basketball?" The coach saw how eager Babe was to learn, so he taught her.

It didn't take long before Babe was ready to go back for another tryout. She made the girls high school basketball team and became its high scorer. She led the team to the state championship in two consecutive years.[2] Babe was named to the all-city and all-state teams.[3] People no longer said she was too small.

Babe played the game very aggressively. She was not afraid to bump other players when going up for rebounds. Driving in for layups, she'd often send defenders crashing to the floor.[4]

In high school, Babe was on every team available to girls—volleyball,

Despite her small size, Babe was determined to play on her high school basketball team.

Babe practices her diving.

tennis, golf, baseball, basketball and swimming. Beatrice Lytle, Babe's gym teacher and one of her coaches at Beaumont High School said: "Babe was the most teachable person I have ever known."[5] A desire to learn is the most critical element in being teachable. When it came to sports, Babe was the most willing of students—in high school and throughout her life.

Many young people like sports and play whatever sports they can. But few are willing to work as hard at it as Babe was. Few are willing to seek out and accept the coaching as Babe did. From her days in school throughout her entire career, Babe sought out the best available coaches and learned all they could teach. Then she spent hour after hour, day after day, practicing what she had learned.

Why commit so much time and energy to sports? One of her friends in Beaumont, Raymond Alford, said he had the same motivation that Babe did. "We were poor," he said of Babe and himself. "The only way to get recognition was through sports. We could hobnob with the rich kids if we stood out in athletics."[6]

Years later, Raymond Alford told a story that illustrated Babe's competitiveness. He was the high school football team's kicker. He would often practice kicking on his own. Sometimes Babe would be there with him. Eventually she began kicking. Soon she challenged her friend, saying: "I can kick better than you." Funny thing was, Raymond said, "she could kick better than I could." Babe went to the football coach and told him she could out-kick Ray and should be on the team. But girls were not allowed on football teams. So that was the end of that.[7]

Raymond Alford understood Babe and admired her, and she felt comfortable with him. But she felt out of place with many of her other neighbors and classmates. At school, she didn't care for academics. She didn't fail any subjects but she never worked very hard to excel in the classroom, as some kids did. And at sports, she was a little too rough for most of the other girl athletes. They would applaud her after a great game then speak unkind things about her behind her back.

And while the boys admired her athletic skills, they often felt overwhelmed by her. Here was this girl who was better than they were in most sports. That was embarrassing to most boys back then. While these boys could cheer Babe's exploits on the basketball court, they didn't ask her out on dates. In many ways, Babe was a hero and an outcast at the same time.[8]

All of the victories, honors, and headlines did little to keep Babe from being lonely. Fortunately she had great support from her family and a few close friends. The only time she felt she "belonged" was when she was with her family or in a sports contest.

◆◆◆

3
Babe Makes Her Move

While Babe was setting scoring records on the Beaumont High School basketball team, her reputation was spreading. One person who helped build her reputation was Bill "Tiny" Scurlock. He was the sports reporter for the local newspaper, the *Beaumont Journal*. He took a liking to Babe and made sure the people of Beaumont knew about her athletic talent. He wrote stories in the paper about every game Babe played. He even wrote stories about her when she wasn't playing. Babe contributed to these stories by filling Tiny in on details of her games when he wasn't there in person. She knew at an early age the power of the press. She knew that good publicity would help her reach her goal of being recognized as the world's greatest athlete.[1]

Eventually Babe's reputation reached Dallas, Texas, and a man by the name of Melvin J. McCombs. He had to see for himself if this girl he had heard about was as good as people said. He went to scout this girl from Beaumont who was dominating high school basketball in the state.

He was called Colonel McCombs. He coached a women's semi-pro basketball team in Dallas called the Golden Cyclones. A semi-pro team usually was made up of players who were no longer in school. Companies sponsored these teams. That is, the companies paid for the uniforms, the equipment, and any travel expenses. Most of the players worked for the company. Though the players didn't get paid for playing, they received a salary for the work they did in an office, factory, or other company facility.

The Golden Cyclones were sponsored by Employer's Casualty Insurance Company. Rather than using its whole name, people referred to it as ECC. Companies like ECC felt that sponsoring these teams helped promote the company name. (Today you see companies sponsoring teams from Little League up through the Olympics.) In a way, sponsoring a semi-pro team was like advertising. The teams played in different cities because women's basketball was popular in Texas in the 1920s and 1930s. So as the team traveled around the state, the company name went with it. When reports of games appeared in the newspapers, the company

Babe with the Employers Casualty basketball team.

received more free "advertising." This kind of publicity helped project a good image of the company.

In 1930, Colonel McCombs went to see Babe play on the Beaumont High School team. One game was all he needed to see. That same day he offered her a job as a stenographer at ECC, if she would play on the company team. (A stenographer takes notes in shorthand as someone speaks and then transcribes the notes into complete words and sentences.)

The company would pay Babe $75 a month for her work as a stenographer. Babe was excited. That was more money than she could have dreamed of. It was so much more than the penny a bag she received at the gunnysack company. It was so much more than her mother made scrubbing other people's clothes. Because she had seen how her family struggled to get by, Babe knew how much her salary could help. And she would be doing what she loved most—playing basketball. She'd be playing basketball with and against the best players in the state. Babe knew she had to play against top competition if she were going to become the greatest athlete that ever lived.

But her parents were hesitant. For one thing, Babe would have to drop out of high school. For another, she would have to move to Dallas and live away from the family. There would be a chaperone to supervise the young players like Babe, but a chaperone is not family.[2]

Hannah and Ole discussed the situation. They finally decided to let Babe go. "We came to this country for the opportunities to advance," Ole said. He and Hannah decided not to stand in the way of Babe's taking advantage of this opportunity to advance.[3]

In her first game for ECC, Babe wore number 7, which she had hoped for. It didn't matter that the pants and shirt were too big for her.[4] No one else seemed to mind either. Babe scored 18 points in that first game. ECC won 48-18. Babe scored as many points as the entire opposing team scored.[5]

With Babe as the leader, the Golden Cyclones piled up win after win. In her first three seasons on the team, Babe was named All-America.[6] In the Amateur Athletic Union (AAU) tournament in Wichita, Kansas, the Cyclones won four games. Then they lost in the finals by one point. Babe scored more than 100 points in the five games.[7]

Babe enjoyed playing on the Cyclones team and working at ECC. She lived, worked, and played among a group of girls and young women who were much like herself. Most of them were eager to play ball. Babe didn't feel like an outsider among them.[8]

But Babe didn't forget her main mission—to become known as the greatest. As she traveled from city to city with the Cyclones, she always bought the local newspaper. She would clip out stories about the game and her play. She would send these back to Tiny Scurlock. He would rework the story and have it printed in the Beaumont Journal. He and Babe wanted to make sure the people of Beaumont knew of every one of her successes. Babe would also send letters to Tiny, filling in details that the original newspaper story had left out. Babe's letters were filled with grammatical mistakes and spelling errors. That was a sign that she hadn't paid as much attention in school as she should have. She was lucky to have Tiny rewrite for her.[9]

Babe quickly learned that being recognized as a superior athlete could pay off in many ways. One was in her paycheck. Other companies with semi-pro teams approached Babe to leave ECC and take a job with them. They offered her better jobs and more money to make the switch. When she approached Colonel McCombs and told him about these offers, he made Babe a different kind of offer. Instead of more money, he offered to train her in other sports.[10]

Colonel McCombs had Babe play on the company's softball team. Then he created a swimming team around her. She competed in various forms of diving as well as swimming. He even gave Babe equal billing with the company. He advertised the swimming team as "Mildred Didrikson and Her Employer's Casualty Girls."[11] That name put Babe prominently before the public. It also was a reminder to Babe and everyone else that she was employed by Employer's Casualty Insurance Company.

As she watched Colonel McCombs use her to promote his company, Babe was learning an important lesson. She realized that for a girl, playing a sport well was not enough. To make the most out of her skills, she would have to promote herself at every opportunity. She would have to place herself in the public eye and make people like what they see.

At one point, Colonel McCombs introduced Babe to track and field. He took her to see her first track meet. When she saw a javelin, she asked, "What's that?"[12] (A javelin is a wooden or metal spear that athletes throw. The athlete who throws the javelin the farthest wins the event.)

McCombs picked up a javelin and threw it. Then Babe did the same. She liked it. He showed her other events—running dashes, high jump, long-jump, hurdles. Babe was hooked. She wanted very much to compete in track and field—in as many events as she could.

Babe applied herself to track and field as she had to basketball. She worked with McCombs to learn the fundamentals. She practiced with the team. Then she practiced on her own for hours and hours. On many occasions she practiced long after dark.

McCombs got to know Babe very well. He knew the kinds of things that could motivate her. For instance, when she was talking about moving to another company for more money, he won her over not with money but with more competition in other sports. Another technique he used was to reward her when she accomplished something special. In their high-jump practices, McCombs would set the bar high. He promised her a chocolate soda if she cleared the bar. When she cleared it, he gave her a soda. Then he would raise the bar still higher. If she cleared that, she'd get another soda. What McCombs didn't tell Babe was that in those practices he was setting the bar at world record heights.[13] He was readying her for world-class competition.

In one of her first meets, Babe competed against Bowen Air Lines in Fort Worth, Texas. That meet was for the Texas State Championship. Babe entered 10 events. She won a medal in eight of the 10. Babe won in the shot put (throwing a heavy metal ball). She won in the discus (throwing a heavy circular plate, usually made of wood with a metal rim). She won in throwing the javelin. She was also first in the broad jump and the high jump. She won the 100-yard dash and the 200-yard dash. She placed second in the 50-yard dash.[14]

To even dare to enter 10 events as a newcomer had to demand a bushel of confidence. Babe indeed was confident. "My main idea," she wrote, "in any kind of competition always has been to go out there and cut loose with everything I've got. I've always had the confidence that I was capable of winning out."[15]

Babe was still concerned that ECC was not paying her what she was worth to the company. To win her over

Representing the ECC, Babe single-handedly took on the AAU National Track and Field championships.

again, Colonel McCombs gave her another opportunity for more publicity. He offered to enter her in the 1932 AAU National Track and Field championships in Evanston, Illinois. She would compete as the only member of the ECC team. Her teammates didn't like the special treatment she was getting. They didn't like her bragging either. But their resentment didn't deter Babe. She saw this meet as a chance to gain publicity at the national level. If she did well, her reputation would extend far beyond Texas. People all across America would know her name. Confident as ever, Babe predicted that as a one-person team, she would win this meet.[16]

The night before the meet, Babe suffered from stomach pains. The team chaperone called a doctor. He diagnosed her pain as a case of nerves. Babe didn't fall asleep until the early morning. As a result, she slept past the normal wake-up time. She was late in getting to the stadium. To save time, she changed in the taxi.[17]

In Evanston, Babe would compete against some of the best athletes in America. It came time to begin. The announcer called out the name of each team, and the team members trotted on to the track. People in the stands applauded. Then the announcer called out "Employer's Casualty Insurance Company." Babe trotted out alone. The crowd roared to see just one person—Babe—taking her position next to all the other teams. Some teams had as many as 25 members. Rather than be embarrassed, Babe soaked in the attention. With a big smile on her face, she waved enthusiastically to the crowd.[18]

As the only member of her team Babe had little or no time to rest between events. For three hours, Babe scurried from one event to another[19]

Babe won six gold medals that day:

- She set a new AAU and U.S. record in the eight-pound shot put at 39 feet, 6 inches
- She set a world record in the baseball throw at 272 feet, 2 inches
- She set a world record in the javelin throw at 139 feet, 3 inches
- She won the 80-yard hurdle race in 12.1 seconds
- She tied for first in the high jump, at 5 feet, 3 inches, an AAU record
- She won the long jump at 17 feet, six inches
- She was fourth in the discus throw[20]

This unequaled display added up to a total of 30 points for the ECC team (Babe). The next closest team—the Illinois Women's Athletic Club, which had 20 members—scored a total of 22 points. By herself, Babe outscored her closest competitors by eight points. Single-handedly, at 20, she won the National AAU championship for ECC.[21]

A United Press reporter, George Kirsey, called Babe's achievement "the most amazing series of performances ever accomplished by any individual, male or female, in track and field history."[22] Babe was on her way toward achieving her goal.

After winning, Babe talked to reporters, something she would do whenever she could. "I told those girls," she

Babe wins the AAU Championship.

said in her brash manner, "Ah'm gonna lick you single-handed." The press loved her "down-home" honesty. Of course, she backed up her boast and that in itself made for a great story.²³

In the autobiography that Babe wrote years later, she described that day in a less boastful manner. "It was just one of those days in an athlete's life when you know you are just right. You feel you could fly. You're like a feather floating on air."²⁴

This spectacular day drew Babe one important step closer to her goal of being known as the greatest athlete. People were now talking about Babe Didrikson outside of Texas.

Winning this National AAU Championship brought Babe an unexpected surprize. Because of her incomparable showing, the scrawny girl from Beaumont was selected to become a member of the 1932 United States Olympic team. Soon the name Babe Didrikson would be familiar to people beyond the boundaries of the United States.

◆◆◆

4
Olympic Hero

Los Angeles, California, was the setting for the 1932 Olympic Games. Babe would not be the only member of this team as she had been in Evanston. She would be teammate to a number of other women. Most of them had been training in track and field much longer than Babe had. But on the train to California, Babe did nothing to endear herself to her teammates.

For one thing, Babe had a habit of boasting. She'd make her teammates feel that she was the star and they were merely supporting cast members. For another, she pulled a number of pranks they didn't like. The most annoying episode came when the train made a stop at Albuquerque, New Mexico. The city's radio station had arranged to have reporters at the train depot to interview each team member on the radio. Each woman was to give her name and hometown. Then she would give a bit of information about herself, her event, or her feeling about being in the Olympics.

Well, Babe stole the show from her teammates. She found a bicycle at the train depot and began riding it up and down in front of the radio reporters. As she rode, she was telling them who she was. She bragged that soon everyone in the country would know the name Babe Didrikson. She even took out her harmonica and began playing it. This bold display made for far more interesting "radio" than the short interviews that had been scheduled. So the reporters stayed with Babe until the train was ready to roll again. Her teammates didn't like being upstaged by Babe. They didn't like being denied their 30 seconds of fame. But that didn't bother Babe. Being liked by her teammates was less important than being recognized throughout the world of sports.

There were reporters on the train, too, and Babe spent much time talking to them. Her message to them was: "I came out here to beat out everybody in sight and that's just what I'm gonna do."[1]

The setting for the 1932 Olympic Games was perfect for someone wanting to get into the national spotlight. Within Los Angeles is Hollywood, the movie capital of the world. Many big name movie stars would attend the games. And so would many of the reporters who follow the stars. Reporters loved movie stars and athletes who cooperated with the press. That made their jobs easier. Reporters also loved an outgoing personality like Babe's. So Babe skillfully used this opportunity to promote herself. She gave the press homespun quotes that showed her to be a simple, hard-working country girl. Here are some of those quotes:

- o "What I want to do most of all in the Olympics is to win four firsts—something no girl has ever done."
- o "Yep, I'm going to win the high jump Sunday and set a world record. I don't know who my opponents are and, anyways, it wouldn't make any difference."

The press hung on her every word. They gave her nicknames such as "Whatta Gal Didrikson," "The Texas Tornado," and "The Terrific Tomboy."[2]

At the opening day ceremonies, even the brash Babe was in awe. More than 100,000 people filled the stands. Flags from all of the participating countries flapped in the breeze. Hundreds of snow white doves were released and flew majestically across the blue sky. Team members from throughout the world marched into the stadium and stood drinking in the spectacle. "It was a wonderful thrill," Babe later wrote, "to march into the Olympic Stadium in the parade on opening day."[3]

Olympic Hero

But Babe quickly became uncomfortable. "We all had to wear special dresses and stockings and white shoes that the Olympic Committee issued to us," she wrote. "I believe that was about the first time I'd ever worn a pair of stockings in my life; I was used to anklets and socks. And as for those shoes, they were really hurting my feet." [4]

Once the festivities ended and the games began, Babe felt comfortable. In those days, there were only five Olympic events for women. Each woman could be entered in only three of the five. Babe chose the javelin throw, 80-meter hurdles, and the high jump.[5] So she could not achieve her goal of four firsts. But she was now in her own element—competitive sports.

Babe's first event was the javelin throw. When she took her position, she saw a small German flag stuck in the ground. That flag marked the spot of the current Olympic record in the javelin throw. It was a German flag because a German woman had set the record. Babe focused on that little flag. She took her position and threw. But for some reason—maybe she hadn't warmed up enough—the javelin slipped. Instead of traveling in an arc, the javelin went out on a flat line. It zipped along "like a catcher's peg from home to second base," Babe later wrote. Usually a javelin thrown in an arc will carry a longer distance. But Babe's throw carried 143 feet, 4 inches. That was about 14 feet past that little flag. Babe set a new world record.[6]

Though she set the record, Babe tore cartilage in her shoulder when her hand slipped. In most track and field events, athletes get three chances. People wondered why Babe's next two javelin tosses weren't close to her first. But she didn't tell anyone about her injury. Fortunately that first toss held up. The German woman who had held the record before Babe came in a close second. Her toss was within nine inches of Babe's.[7] That's one gold medal for Babe.

Two days later, Babe ran in the 80-meter hurdles. In this race, runners are assigned to compete in "heats," or groups. One group runs, then another, and possibly a third. Only the top two runners in each group qualify to compete against one another for the medal.

The Olympic record for this event had been 12.2 seconds. In her first heat, Babe's time was 11.8 seconds. She set another new Olympic record. The next day, Babe lined up against all of the qualifiers in the finals. Eager for another win, she jumped the gun. That means she began running before the starter gave the signal. Other runners broke and they all had to resume their position. If she jumped the gun a second time, Babe would be disqualified. Not wanting to jump the gun again, Babe hung back. She was left behind by the others who took off at the crack of the starter's gun. Babe had to make up ground—quickly. She caught up to the leaders at the fifth hurdle. Then she won by a whisker. Her time— 11.7 seconds. That was one-tenth of a second better than her time on the first day. She set another new Olympic record.[8] She won her second gold medal in her second event. One more to go.

Olympic Hero

Babe sets an Olympic record and wins a gold medal in the 80-meter hurdles.

After each day's events, swarms of reporters gathered around Babe for her thoughts and comments. After winning the gold in the 80-meter hurdle, Babe told reporters about how she hurdled hedges back home in Beaumont.[9] Her "hedgehopping" made great fodder for the next day's newspapers. It was just the kind of story the reporters loved to write and the kind that readers loved to read.

Babe's third event was the high jump. After the preliminaries, Babe competed for the gold medal against one of her American teammates, Jean Shiley. The bar was set at 5 feet, 5 inches. That was two inches higher than the record Babe had set in Evanston. Both Jean and Babe cleared the bar. For the next jump, the bar was raised to 5 feet, 6 inches. Jean went first and missed getting across. With an opportunity to win her third gold medal in three events, Babe ran and took off. She cleared the bar. But as

Clearing the bar of the high jump.

she landed on the other side, her foot hit the standard. The bar came tumbling down. Babe's pass did not count.

For the third jump, the bar was lowered to 5 feet, 5 $\frac{1}{4}$ inches. If either woman cleared the bar, she would set a new Olympic and world record. Jean went first and made it. She cleared the bar. The pressure was now on Babe. If she failed to clear, Jean would win the gold. Babe took her position and focused all of her attention on the bar. She went into her trot and then ran. She lifted herself off the ground and over the bar. She made it.[10]

But then the judges quickly gathered together to confer. They decided that Babe's jump was illegal. They said she dived over the bar, with her head going first. That style was called the "Western roll."[11] Today that wouldn't matter. But at the time, the Western roll was not allowed in the Olympic games. Babe said that was the way she had always jumped. But the judges declared Jean Shiley the gold medal winner. Babe won the silver.

Babe was disappointed. Her disappointment didn't last long, however. She had won two gold medals and a silver. Reporters wrote glowingly about this phenomenal display of athletic ability. And about this brash, honest young woman from Texas. They coined more nicknames such as "Belting Babe" and "Iron Woman".[12]

She told the reporters about her upbringing in a very poor family. She described her mother's taking in laundry. She talked about the family's eating onion sandwiches when they couldn't afford anything else. She described how she herself worked as a youngster in the burlap factory earning one cent for each bag she sewed.[13]

The country was heading into an economic depression in 1932. Many people were out of work and poor. Reading about this poor girl who "made it big" gave people hope. They loved reading about Babe. And the reporters couldn't get enough of Babe. They gave her another name "our Babe."

Among the writers present at these Olympic Games was Grantland Rice. He was one of the most influential of all sports writers. He wrote the lines that have become so famous:

> "For when the One Great Scorer comes to mark
> against your name, He writes—not that you won or lost—
> but how you played the game."[14]

Grantland Rice admired Babe. And he told her he thought she should have been given an equal share of the gold medal for the high jump. He invited her to play golf the next day.[15] Though golf was not yet her game, Babe accepted the invitation. Babe loved the spotlight and publicity. She was not about to pass up an opportunity to spend time with such an important member of the press.

While Babe, the Olympic champion, basked in the glory of her victory, other Olympians had a much tougher time of it. Athletes at the time were not treated as royally as they are today. Some athletes could not attend the big post-games party because the Olympic committee would

Olympic Hero

Babe wins two gold medals and one silver medal at the 1932 Olympics.

not pay for one more night at a hotel. Jean Shiley, who won the gold, cashed in her train ticket and bought a less expensive bus ticket home. That was the only way she could get enough money to buy a few souvenirs for her family. Another teammate had to give up her car because she could not afford the payments on it.[16] These were all first-class athletes. Some of them, like Jean Shiley, were medal winners. But Babe was "the story," because of her winning three medals in three events. And because she knew how to "work" the press.

Babe's trip home was different from that of her teammates. She still had her job at ECC, which sponsored her in the Olympics. They paid for an airline ticket so Babe could fly back to Texas in style. Fifteen US Army planes escorted Babe's plane into Dallas. When her plane landed, she heard marching bands and saw crowds of people there to greet her. Her family was there. So were her ECC teammates from the Golden Cyclones. Then Babe was honored with a parade through downtown Dallas. She got to ride in the police chief's car. At a luncheon in her honor, the mayor and other dignitaries paid tribute to Babe. Radio stations carried the entire event over the air to Babe's many fans.[17]

Two days later, Babe received a hero's welcome from her hometown of Beaumont. Among the many honors bestowed on her, perhaps the most meaningful came from the Beaumont High School principal. He pleased the crowd and Babe when he said: "Your school record will be changed from 'withdrew February 14, 1930' to 'left school to be the world's greatest athlete.'"[18]

It wasn't only her friends, neighbors, and families who admired Babe's Olympic feat. Grantland Rice, who was around star athletes most of his life, wrote about Babe:

> She is an incredible human being. She is beyond belief until you see her perform. Then you finally understand that you are looking at the most flawless section of muscle harmony, of complete mental and physical coordination the world of sport has ever known. This may seem to be a wild statement, yet it happens to be 100 percent true. There is only one Babe Didrikson and there has never been another in her class—even close to her class.[19]

5

Babe's Fall From Grace

After her Olympic triumph, Babe was big news—for a short time. Amelia Earhart, the famous pilot, asked Babe to join her on one of her flights. Amelia thought Babe's presence would bring good publicity to the flight. Reports circulated that Hollywood offered Babe movie contracts. She did, in fact, make a 10-minute film in which she throws the javelin, the discus, and the shot put; soars in the high jump and the long jump; sprints; hurdles; swims; dives; hits golf and tennis balls; plays basketball; pitches and hits a baseball; and passes and punts a football. The title of that film was "The Wonder Girl."[1]

But then things began to turn in the wrong direction for Babe. In 1933, an ad appeared in the *Chicago Daily News* showing a picture of Babe and a Dodge automobile. The ad had words suggesting that Babe was endorsing the car. That is, it seemed as though Babe was saying: "This is a good car and you should buy it." The AAU saw the ad and concluded Babe must have been paid for it. That payment violated her amateur status. Babe would not be allowed to compete in AAU events, such as the one in Evanston that she won single-handedly. The Dodge dealer swore that Babe had not been paid. Some time later, the AAU offered to reinstate Babe but she did not accept the offer. She decided that she would earn some money.[2] She would give up her amateur status and turn pro.

But there were not many opportunities for women athletes to earn a living at sports. And Babe did have to earn her own living. She was no longer employed at ECC.

One way she earned money was by signing a contract to promote Chrysler cars. Companies today still promote their products through the voice (and face) of star athletes. Another way Babe earned money was by performing in a stage show. Babe stood on a theater stage and told jokes, played her harmonica, ran on a treadmill, and did a series of athletic exercises. For a whole week, people packed the theater and loved Babe's act. The producers offered her a large sum of money—$2500 a week—to do the show in different towns. But Babe turned them down. She said she didn't want to be cooped up inside. She wanted to work outdoors.[3]

Babe put together Babe Didrikson's All Americans. This was a basketball team of men and women. Over a five-month period, the team played 91 games, each in a different town. Babe was playing sports, which she loved, but the travel wore her down.

Babe even resorted to doing novelty exhibitions for pay. One of these involved the House of David, a men's professional baseball team. All of the players wore long beards. The team hired Babe to pitch a few innings at each game. As an added attraction, Babe got more fans to buy tickets to the games.

These kinds of activities had to be demeaning for Babe. She was an Olympic champion. Not long before, she had been the reigning queen of sports. Now people saw her as little more than a sideshow. In one game she played baseball while riding on a donkey.[4] One reporter wrote: "At an age when most people are wondering when the first break is going to come, Mildred Didrikson is one of the most illustrious has-beens."[5] ("Has-been" is a term used for a person who once was a celebrity but no longer is.)

Besides being demeaning, these activities left Babe lonely. The House of David team would play in one town today and then move to another town for another game tomorrow, much like a traveling carnival. Babe didn't travel with the team. After pitching her few innings, she'd get in her car and drive ahead to the next town—by herself. In one year, 1934, Babe pitched in 200 games with this team. That meant 200 solitary automobile trips and 200 lonely nights in dreary hotels. The physical and emotional drain was great.

At an exhibition game with Ruth McGinnis, women's professional pocket billiards champion.

But Babe grew up in a time when people did what had to be done to make a living. She had seen first-hand how her parents struggled. She had never been pampered and she was not the type to pamper herself. So she sucked it up and did what she had to do. She didn't make much money and she gave much of what she did earn to her parents. When her father became very sick, the family had to take him to a charity hospital in Galveston, Texas. They could not afford the hospital closer to home. This incident made Babe even more determined to earn money. [6]

Negative press added to Babe's woes. For some time, the press—which once adored Babe—had become critical of her. Some reporters wrote stories that she was "not-quite-female," not feminine enough to suit Americans. Some said she was "boyish-looking." She didn't wear frilly clothes or cut her hair stylishly. A reporter for the *New York World-Telegram*, Joe Williams, wrote: "It would be much better if she and her ilk (type) stayed at home, got themselves prettied up and waited for the phone to ring."[7] It was just this kind of sexist attitude that Babe was trying to combat.

Women, too, had not gotten used to the idea of female athletes. Some used Babe to show "the harm sports can do." Such women said that Babe's barnstorming around the country, did not help her reputation. Nor did it help women's sports.[8] Mothers would say things like: "I don't want my daughters playing sports. They might wind up like this Babe—manly and un-feminine and traipsing across the country with who-knows-what."

People criticized Babe for playing "manly sports" that involved running, jumping, throwing, and sports that involved body contact, like basketball. They preferred "beautiful" sports for women, such as golf, ice-skating, and swimming.[9]

Babe's friend, Tiny Scurlock, and some other writers tried to counter these attitudes with stories about Babe showing her "feminine" side. They wrote about her once sewing a dress in school that won an award. Stories

Babe's "boyish" appearance caused some to criticize her unfairly.

appeared about her house-keeping and a large pink hat that she bought.[10] But these efforts were not enough.

What a strange situation. Here was the greatest woman athlete in the world being made the victim of prejudice.[11]

Never one to take things lying down, Babe decided to do something that would revive her career and popularity. It would also earn her money. She would take up golf.

◆◆◆

6

Babe Climbs Back to The Top

In the 1930s, golf was one of the few sports considered appropriate for "a lady." It didn't involve being physical, as there was no running or jumping. Golfers didn't get dirty or perspire much. And the women could wear fashionable, feminine clothing. Another reason women may not have been discouraged from golf was that wealthy women played golf. Unlike today, there were very few public golf courses in the 1930s. The only people who played the sport did so at exclusive country clubs. To become a member of such a club cost a good deal of money. People were less likely to criticize wealthy women playing golf than criticize poor women playing basketball.[1]

For these and other reasons, women had been playing golf in the United States for many years. In 1900, Margaret Abbot became the first American woman to win a gold medal in golf at the Olympic Games. Women's softball did not become a medal sport in the Olympic Games until 1996. By then, golf had been part of women's Olympics for more than 100 years. That gap in time shows the difference in attitudes towards a "manly" sport like softball and a "ladylike" sport like golf. (You can learn more about women's softball in the Olympic Games in the Girls Explore book *Go for It!*, by Dot Richardson, Olympic Gold Medalist and Orthopedic Surgeon.)

You may recall that Babe was invited to play golf with Grantland Rice, the senior sports writer in America. At the 1932 Olympic Games he was raving about Babe's natural athletic ability. He made the statement that she would be good at any sport. "How about golf?" someone asked. It was more a challenge than a question. "Even golf," Rice shot back. So he invited Babe to play with him and his friends the next day. Records disagree on her score that day. Some say she hit drives of 250 yards. Whatever the actual figures, Babe performed well enough for the other players to admit that Rice was right. She could play the game.[3]

So after trying other approaches to making a living and rebuilding her reputation, Babe turned to golf. She was then 21 years-old. Today's successful golfers—men and women—generally begin playing golf seriously in their early teens. Often they start earlier than that. So 21 was old to be starting to learn to play golf—to be good enough to play it at a championship level. And Babe would not consider any other level.

In the fall of 1933, Babe, with her mother and sister, went to California to become a professional golfer. She took lessons from one of the most respected pros (instructors) in the game, Stan Kertes. The first thing Kertes taught Babe was the grip. When she held the golf club, she held it with her fists, as if it were a baseball bat. Kertes had to work with her to get her to hold the club with her fingers.

As she had done in other sports, Babe devoted herself

Babe took lessons with the famous golfer Stan Kertes.

to mastering the golf swing. After taking a lesson, Babe would stay at the range hitting golf balls. She hit 1000 balls every day. On some days she hit 1500. She would stay at the range for eight to 10 hours a day. Sometimes she'd go home with her hands blistered and bleeding.[4]

Babe had natural ability, but she knew she could not rely on that alone. Like most champions, she put in hours and years of hard work to draw out every bit of natural ability.

In 1934, Babe played in her first golf tournament. It was the Fort Worth Women's Open, in Fort Worth, Texas. Newspaper reporters from across the state and other states came to see if the Olympian of two years past could play this game. Babe must have been glad to see them. Though she was new at the game, Babe carried herself as she always had. When a reporter asked, "How do you think you'll do?" Babe answered, "I think I'll shoot a 77." And that's exactly what Babe shot—77. In the next round she shot an 82. Babe faltered somewhat in the following round and was eliminated. But she had made an impressive start. She would need more lessons and more practice. But she was already looking ahead to the Texas State Women's Championship in the spring of 1935.[5]

To prepare for that tournament, Babe played with and learned from one of the best golfers of the time—Gene Sarazen. That arrangement came about through her friend, the sports writer Grantland Rice. He suggested that Gene and Babe play a series of exhibitions against one another.[6] That would give Babe an opportunity to earn some money, practice her game under regulation conditions, and learn as much as she could from one of the best.

Babe made the most of this opportunity. She repeatedly asked Gene about how to play different shots and how to handle certain clubs. Sometimes she'd ask these questions during an exhibition. Sometimes Gene gave her private lessons. Even here, Babe was promoting herself. Before some of these lessons, Babe would tip off the sports writers that she and Gene would be at a certain place at a certain time.[7] Reporters would show up—with photographers—and Babe would be back in the sports pages.

But Babe was serious about learning to play. After working with her for two months, Gene said: "I only know of one golfer who practiced more than Babe and that was Ben Hogan."[8] In the minds of many, Ben Hogan may have been the best male golfer of all time—past and present.

During the exhibition rounds themselves, Babe worked the people in the gallery. Most golfers like complete silence when they play. But Babe didn't. She chatted and chattered with the fans. She'd tell jokes and funny stories. She'd do tricks with the golf club and ball. Gene said: "Babe liked to play to the crowd. That's why she never developed a real sweet swing. She always wanted to powder it—to please the fans."

The fans enjoyed her kidding during a match. In earshot of the crowd she'd say to Gene: "Squire, what (club) are you using here?" "A five," he'd say. "Then I'll use a seven," Babe would say, to the delight of the crowd. (By using a seven, Babe was showing that she could hit the ball farther than Gene could.)[9]

In all, Babe and Gene played 18 exhibition matches together. In some matches they competed against each other. In other matches they teamed up against another twosome. Babe achieved both of her goals. She made money and she polished up her skills.

Babe was now back in the public eye and companies took notice. A sporting goods company offered Babe a contract agreement. If she would use only its golf equipment, the company would pay her $25,000 a year.[10]

When she wasn't playing golf with Gene Sarazen or taking lessons, Babe was back at work at ECC. She had returned to the company that gave her her first break. She was now a publicist for the company. (That means she would speak for the company and represent it at various functions.) But Babe would devote her lunch hour to practicing her putting on the carpet in the office. She would leave work at 5:30 and head straight for the driving range. She hit bucket after bucket of golf balls until her hands bled. She'd go home and have dinner. Then she'd go to bed reading a book on the rules of golf.

Babe felt it was important to know all of the rules of the sport you play. And to follow them. Once in a match Babe accidentally played someone else's ball. She realized it only after the hole was completed and she was washing the ball. She disqualified herself. "You have to play by the rules of golf," she wrote, "just as you have to play by the rules of life."[11]

After all of her practicing, Babe applied to play in the Texas State Women's Golf Championship in Houston. She would be competing against the best golfers in the state. But the Texas Women's Golf Association would not approve her

Practice makes perfect: Babe works hard to master the rules and technique of golf.

application. The Association said she didn't have the credentials. They said she would have to establish herself in other tournaments before she could be allowed to compete in this major tournament. Why the Association didn't want Babe to play is anyone's guess. But the comments of one Association member gives some idea of why. The member said: "We don't need any truck driver's daughter in this tournament."[12]

Prejudice was again rearing its ugly head. Wasn't this America, where everyone is considered equal? Did it matter that Babe came from a poor family? Wasn't the important thing how well she could play the game?

Babe had the last laugh, however. She reminded the committee that she was a member of the Beaumont Country Club in her home town. (Babe's Olympic triumphs enabled her to become a member.) As a member of a club that was in Texas, she had a right to play in the Texas State Women's Golf Tournament. Having no choice, the committee allowed Babe to play.[13]

But the displays of prejudice continued. On the day before the first round of play, golfers competed in a driving contest. When Babe arrived at the range, some of the other golfers withdrew from the driving contest. Rather than get angry, Babe took another approach to dealing with this unfounded hostility. To counter the criticism that she was too "manly" or "too muscular," she poked fun at their idea of femininity. She preened and pranced and took ridiculous, weak swings. She purposely hit a few balls weakly into the ground.[14] She mocked their "ladylike" idea. She made her point.

Once she was satisfied that everybody got the idea, Babe stepped up to the tee. She took a swing and blasted a ball 250 yards.

Then things got serious. Babe played well and made it into the semi-finals. The course was wet with heavy rain. Babe won that match by one stroke. She would play the next day in the finals for the championship. Her opponent was Peggy Chandler, considered the best in women's golf.

The scoring for the tournament was based on the number of holes a player won, not the total score. The golfers would play two rounds or 36 holes.

Babe and Peggy were tied after 33 holes. On the 34th, Babe outdrove Peggy off the tee. Peggy's second shot was short of the green. If Babe shot to the green, she would have a better chance of making birdie or par than Peggy would. That is, Babe would get the ball in the hole in fewer strokes. But Babe hit her second shot over the green. Not only did her shot go over the green; her ball landed in a roadway, in a small ditch filled with water. Peggy chipped up to the green, close to the hole. She had a relatively easy birdie (one under par, the standard for the hole) putt facing her. Meanwhile, Babe was looking at her ball in this water-filled rut.

"Now, Babe," she said to herself. "Take your time and play this one right." She later wrote in her autobiography that she went through all of the things she had been taught about making a difficult shot like the one she would have to make. She thought about how to stand and how to hold the club. Most importantly, she reminded herself about the first rule of golf: "Look at the ball real good."

Babe swung. The ball went spinning up onto the green and toward the pin. People went rushing up. Babe could no longer see the ball but she heard the crowd roar. The ball had gone into the hole. Her score for the hole was three. That was two under par for the hole. That's called an eagle, a very rare happening. Peggy could not do better than a four. Babe won the hole to go one up with two holes left to play.[15]

Peggy and Babe tied on the 35th. Babe won the 36th and last hole. She won the match by two holes. After playing golf for only two years, Babe won the Texas State Women's Golf Championship.

But the thrill of victory didn't last very long. The girl from the poor family was champion in a country club

Babe, the "tough kid" from Beaumont, competed against Peggy Chandler, a wealthy sophisticate and champion amateur golfer.

sport. Poor people, as well as many others, were happy for Babe. But there were some, mostly the "wealthy sophisticates," who muttered their disapproval. Some members of the Texas Women's Golf Association complained that Babe should be disqualified. Because she was a professional in other sports—that is, she had received pay for playing baseball, for instance—she should not have been allowed to participate in an amateur event. This tournament was such an event. The United States Golf Association concurred. It ruled Babe ineligible to play in any more amateur golf tournaments. So not only was she banned from amateur golf in Texas; but she was also banned across the United States. That meant she would be able to compete in only one major tournament—the Western Open. That tournament was for amateurs and professionals.[16] First it was the AAU who disqualified her and now the USGA was doing the same.

Babe had used her sense of humor to overcome the snide remarks made about her before the tournament. But then the tough kid from Beaumont took over. She later wrote about that incident: "When you get a big setback like that there's no use crying about it....You have to face your problem and figure out what to do next."[17]

Babe was also smart in the way she dealt with the press. When they asked her how she felt about being ruled ineligible by the USGA, Babe didn't rant and rave, she was more mature now. Instead she responded in a way that made her even more popular with her fans. She said: "Of course, I was disappointed when they told me I couldn't compete as an amateur, but I admire them for barring me, too. They were big enough to adhere to their rules."[18]

While Babe was gracious, her loyal fans across the country were outraged. Some sports writers and a number of men golfers spoke up on Babe's behalf. They were letting the world at large know that the Association had treated Babe unfairly. So instead of being the subject of ridicule, Babe was now the sympathetic underdog. The USGA buckled under the public relations pressure. The Association would allow Babe back into amateur competition if she did not accept any money in connection with sports for three years.[19]

Babe said, "Thanks, but no thanks." She decided she would turn pro. Wilson Sporting Goods Company signed her to promote their equipment. She was getting ready for the Western Open. And Babe had ideas for the future. "As it all turned out," she said, "I'm very happy. My new job (with Wilson) thrills me and I know that women's golf has a greater future in this country than men's. Golf is a game of coordination, rhythm, and grace. Women have this to a much higher degree than men, as dancing shows."[20] Imagine. The brash boyish Babe was praising women's coordination, rhythm, and grace.

Though she put up a good front, Babe was crushed. But she was not one to sit around and brood. Nor was she one to ignore the facts. She realized her image was hurting her career. If she wanted to play golf, she would have to change her image. To get more people to pay more money to watch her play, she would have to be more conventional. That is, she would have to be more lady-like.

She turned for help to Bertha Bowens and her husband

Babe, showing off her graceful, feminine side.

R.L. This wealthy couple was very influential in Texas golf. They understood Babe's situation and agreed that she needed to work on her image. And they offered to teach her. Babe had learned different sports—basketball, baseball, javelin, hurdles, golf. She now was undertaking what may have been her biggest challenge—learning how to be a lady.

The Bowens treated her like a daughter. She moved in with them for a time. They taught her how to be more gentle in her manner. How to carry herself in social company. How to stand and walk. Bertha Bowens worked with Babe on her clothing, getting her to wear more fashionable women's clothing. Bertha took Babe to the hair salon for a softer, more feminine hairstyle. The Bowens took her to meet their friends.

Some of those friends criticized Bertha for befriending Babe. "Why are you fooling with that girl?" they'd say. "It made me so mad," Bertha later said. "Sure, Babe could be crude," she added, "but around those ladies she was very timid. I don't know how she did it but Babe never held a grudge about all that. I never heard her say a bad word about anyone. She did want to do things right."

To her credit, Babe tolerated these lessons and changes. She knew the Bowens were helping her do what she needed to do. And her efforts paid off.

When sportswriter Paul Gallico saw her after she had gone through this make-over, he wrote: "I hardly knew Babe Didrikson. Hair frizzed and she had a neat little wave in it, parted and prettily combed...a touch of rouge

Posing for a portrait, Babe works on changing her image.

(make-up) on her cheeks and red on her lips. The tomboy had suddenly grown up."

Two years later, another writer, Henry McLemore, saw her and wrote: "Her hair is worn in a soft brown, curly cluster about her face. Her figure is that of a Parisian model. Her tweeds (clothing) have the casual authority of New Bond Street and her red nails were a creation of Charles of the Ritz," (both high-priced, first-class places.)[21]

The tomboy look was gone.

♦♦♦

7
Babe Marries George Zaharias

Babe became a pro golfer but there were very few women pros to compete against. So Babe played in a number of exhibitions. At one, she met George Zaharias. They took a liking to each other. After a short courtship, they were married.

George was big, strong, and handsome. Like Babe, he had come from a poor immigrant family. He had been out on his own at a very young age. He worked at whatever odd jobs he could find. One day when he was flat broke, he saw a sign: "Wrestlers wanted—one dollar a day." One dollar a day wasn't much but it was more than nothing a

George Zaharias as a young man

day. So George applied. The job turned out to be a natural for him. He made a career out of it.

Professional wrestling is more theater than sport. The promoters and the two wrestlers arrange ahead of time how the match will go. They determine who will knock down whom, when, and how. The fans know that the match and the outcomes are staged. But they enjoy seeing how it all unfolds.

In most of these matches there is not only a winner and a loser. There is also a good guy and a bad guy. The fans worry when the good guy is down and cheer when he turns the tables on his opponent. And they love to boo and hiss the villain.

George Zaharias made a very good living being a villain in the wrestling ring. He cheated and pulled dirty tricks, all of which the crowd could see. They booed him mercilessly. Then at the designated time, the good guy pinned George. The referee ruled the good guy the winner, the people cheered and went home happy, and George collected a nice paycheck.[1]

After they married, Babe and George went on a six-month honeymoon to Australia and New Zealand. But the trip wasn't all honeymoon. George felt that because no one in these countries had ever seen him or Babe, they would pay to do so. George arranged wrestling matches for himself and golf tournaments or exhibitions for Babe. She was not keen on working during her honeymoon, but she realized these exhibitions would be good for her career. She appreciated George's ability to plan ahead like that. Eventually he gave up wrestling to manage Babe's career and her business affairs. ²

After a short courtship, Babe and George Zaharias finally wed.

Back in the United States, Babe and George decided they had to make a change in her career direction. Because there were so few pro tournaments to play in, they decided to take up the USGA's offer. Babe applied for reinstatement as an amateur. The USGA accepted her application, but she would have to wait three years. During that time she could not play for pay.³

Rather than stay idle, Babe began playing tennis. She took lessons and practiced in her normal manner—until her hands bled or she could no longer stand. But when she applied for admission in the United States Ladies Tennis Association, her application was rejected. The USLTA said Babe was ineligible to play in this organization's tournaments, which were for amateurs only. Though Babe had never been paid for playing tennis, she had been paid for playing other sports. That was enough, the Association said, to rule her out.[4]

Another sport that Babe enjoyed for a while was bowling. This sport had become popular in the late 1930s and early 1940s. George was thinking of buying a bowling alley. When he went looking at alleys that might be for sale, Babe often went along. She saw people bowling and thought she'd try. As might be expected, she liked the sport. She began playing and became quite good. She bowled with a team in the Southern California Major League. In little time, she brought her average up to 170. Her high game was 237—that's out of a possible 300. Not bad for a newcomer.[5]

Of course, golf remained Babe's passion. She practiced often and played in the only two tournaments for which she was eligible—the Texas and Western Opens. She won both tournaments in the same year, 1940. That probably sent a message to the golfing world. "When I become eligible for other tournaments, you'd better watch out."

In December, 1941, the United States entered World War II. Many men went into the military. Many women did, too, though not in combat positions. With so many men in service, women took over their jobs. They worked in offices and factories; they ran farms and stores. Many sports events were cancelled. Celebrities from the worlds of

Babe mastered every sport she tried—even bowling.

sports and entertainment gave their time and talent to help sell war bonds. (These were investments people made that helped provide funds for the government to pay for the war effort.) George put on wrestling matches for the soldiers. Babe participated in many golf exhibitions and matches with celebrities and golf stars such as Ben Hogan.

Babe, of course, didn't limit herself to just playing. She often entertained the crowds with her tricks. One involved her lining up five golf balls on the tee. She rapidly hit one after the other so all five were in the air before the first one hit the ground. For another trick she would tee up two balls. She'd hit one down the fairway and hit the other so it popped up straight and into her pocket. She performed a third trick on the green. She'd lay a number of golf clubs on the green, between her ball and the cup. She would then putt the ball in such a way that it would hop over each of the clubs. Then the ball would roll into the cup.[6]

By 1943, Babe was back in good standing with the USGA. Before playing any sanctioned matches, however, she played a charity match in Palm Springs, California. Her opponent was Clara Callender, the state champion. Babe won the two-round match. She shot a 70 in the first round and a 67 in the second. That two-day total set a record at the Desert Golf Club. A week later she won again at a Los Angeles country club. Then in the summer of 1944 she won the Western Open in Indianapolis.

In 1945, she competed in the Western Open for the third time. She had won the previous two years. No one had ever won this tournament three years in a row. Of course, Babe saw that as an added incentive to play well and win. She knew the road to being declared the best required doing what no one had ever done before. This tournament, however, was particularly grueling for Babe. It also shows the spunk she had.

After the first round, Babe's sister, Esther, called. Their mother had suffered a heart attack. Babe said she'd leave for home immediately. Esther told her not to. "Mama wants you to stay and finish the tournament," Esther said. Babe won the next round the following day. She had another call. Her mother had died. "But don't come home, now," Esther said. "Mama would want you to finish what you started." Babe went out the next day with a heavy heart. There was no chatting with the crowd. There were no jokes. She just did what she had to do. And she won. After the tournament she could not celebrate. Babe left immediately for home. Because of the war situation, getting passage on planes was difficult. It took Babe two days to get home. She made it just in time for her mother's funeral. That day just happened to be Babe's 34th birthday.[7]

◆◆◆

8
Babe Hits Her Stride

When the war ended in 1945, sports events played a major role in bringing the country back to normal. Many activities that had been canceled or scaled back were once again in full swing. That included women's golf.

Babe continued the winning ways. The former Olympic gold medal winner was now known as a golfer—perhaps the best golfer of all time. The Associated Press named Babe the Outstanding Woman Athlete of the Year for 1945.

She had received the same award in 1932 after her Olympic triumph. What a rare feat to win this award 13 years apart, to win for the second time when she was 13 years older, and to win in a totally different kind of sport.

Not only was Babe being recognized for her athletic ability and competitive spirit. People who got close to her realized she was a warm, genuine human being. Peggy Bell, a golfer against whom Babe often competed, was won over when she came to know the real Babe. Babe had asked Peggy to be her playing partner in a Florida tournament and Peggy accepted. Later this is what Peggy said:

> By the time I met Babe, she was not tough or manly. Sometimes she overdressed a little—she'd wear frilly blouses that didn't look right. She was best in tailored things. She could go anywhere. Golf was a more social sport then than now and it lifted Babe up. It made her appreciate the good things in life. She was so proud of being a golfer. She never even talked about the Olympics or all her other sports.[1]

In 1946, Babe established herself as being in a class by herself. She won 17 tournaments in a row. That is a record no other golfer—woman or man—ever equaled before or since. For more than a year, Babe won every tournament she played in.[2]

Though Babe enjoyed playing golf and winning all of these tournaments, she longed to spend some time at home. Golfers have to travel to play tournaments. Babe usually traveled alone. George was busy managing her career and their investments. He didn't want to leave. He would make all of the arrangements and then send Babe off. She spent many a night all alone in a hotel. She wanted to be at home, with George. She wanted time to plant flowers and tend her garden. She wanted to decorate the home she had come to love. She didn't want to stop playing. She just wanted to take a little break.[3]

But George would always persuade her that she had to "strike while the iron's hot." He told her she had to take advantage of her success and popularity. She had a great opportunity to build on her success, to become known as the greatest. "You don't want to let that opportunity slip by," he must have said. Babe would agree, and off she'd go.

One of the events George convinced her to participate in was the 1947 British Women's Amateur championship. Since its inception in 1893, no American had ever won this tournament. That kind of challenge always appealed to Babe—to be the first. So despite the long trip involved—crossing the Atlantic Ocean by ship—Babe went off. How pleasantly surprised she was when she arrived in the town of Gullane, Scotland, where the tournament was held. The people greeted her as if she were a queen. Though she was a foreigner, everyone on the street seemed to recognize her and wish her well. The chef at the hotel where she stayed even brought in special food just for Babe.[4]

The golf course used for the tournament was unlike any Babe had ever played before. The grass was long and damp. And sheep were allowed to roam freely about the course. A man walked ahead of the golfers picking up the sheep droppings. Babe hadn't expected the high grass or the sheep but she took both in stride. She was a good sport about it all.

Babe and her fans at the 1947 British Women's Amateur championship.

Another thing Babe had not expected was cold, damp weather. Babe didn't bring clothes for that kind of weather. On the course for the practice round, Babe was shivering. The next day bundles arrived at her hotel addressed to Babe. She opened the bundles and found fresh warm clothing. The local citizens had learned of her plight and sent her more suitable clothing. Babe selected all she needed and gave the rest to charity, as there were more clothes than she could wear in a week. Babe let the press and the public know she would call the trousers she wore her "lucky pants."[5]

Scoring for the tournament was done by counting the number of holes each golfer won. Babe won the first round easily. And she won over the crowd as she chatted with them. They had never seen a golfer talk with the crowd, much less tell jokes.

In the second round, she won after 16 holes. But rather than go into the clubhouse, Babe said she would play out 17 and 18 just for fun. That delighted the crowd. At the 17th, she teed up a ball and stood a wooden match flush against it. She swung her club and hit the ball about 300 yards as the match flared up. The crowd roared. When Babe, followed by this ecstatic throng, reached her ball, they found it in a sandtrap. Hitting a golf ball out of sand is one of the most difficult shots to make. But not for Babe. She placed a second ball in the sand next to the first one. Then she swung her club. The first ball popped up and she caught it in her pocket. The second ball hopped onto the green and rolled into the cup. The fans broke out into uncontrollable cheering.

Then on the 18th green, she looked over what might be her last shot of the day. She lined up her putt, then all of a sudden she turned around. She straddled the ball and hit the ball from between her legs.

These tricks were this charming lady's way of saying "Thank you" for the hospitality these kind strangers had shown her. They all went home with stories to tell about the great Babe.[6]

When Babe stood at the first tee to begin a two-round final, the crowd was larger than it had been the day before. In fact, more people attended this match than had attended the men's matches two weeks before. Babe and her opponent were tied after the first 18 holes but then Babe won easily in the second round. Observers couldn't tell who was more thrilled with her win—Babe or her fans.

After the match, reporters and photographers gathered around her for pictures and comments. When the photographers asked her to go to the more picturesque front of the clubhouse for pictures, Babe sprinted there, hurdling a low brick wall as she had hurdled the hedges back in Beaumont as a young girl. She did a dance. She sang a Scottish song.[7] Babe had an audience and she loved it. And the audience loved her.

The newspapers all across the world carried stories of Babe's "first-ever" accomplishment—the first American woman to win the British Open. And they regaled at the

Babe and George celebrate her victory.

way in which she did it. They could not say enough about this pleasant, charming, friendly woman. *The Manchester Guardian*, an English newspaper, wrote:

> Surely no woman golfer has accomplished in a championship what Mrs. Zaharias has achieved in this one. She has lost only four holes in six rounds and her score for the holes she played yesterday and today approximates to an average of fours over a course that measures 6600 yards.[8]

The first American woman to win the British Open, Babe shows off her trophy with a bright smile.

When Babe's ship left the port at Edinburgh, Scotland, hundreds of people were at the dock to wave good-bye to her. Some two weeks later, as her ship, the Queen Mary,

A warm welcome: Babe returns home and receives the key to the city from the mayor.

was about three miles outside New York harbor, a tug boat came out to greet the ship. On it were reporters, photographers, and her husband George. After ceremonies in New York, she and George flew home. There Babe was honored with a parade complete with floats and bands. The mayor gave her the key to the city. Babe was indeed back. [9]

◆◆◆

9
Woman Of the Year

Following her triumphal return, Babe was besieged with offers. They were more than George could handle. So she hired a professional agent, Fred Corcoran. To capitalize immediately on Babe's popularity, Corcoran booked Babe into major league stadiums to do a little routine before baseball games. Usually she'd field grounders or throw a few pitches. At this point it didn't matter what Babe did. The fans would be thrilled just to see her. And plenty of fans came to see her.[1]

Babe also gave a number of golfing exhibitions. Over a three-year period she gave 656 exhibitions. That's one every day-and-a-half. For her efforts Babe earned $250,000—that's a quarter of a million dollars. She was drawing higher fees for her exhibitions than her counterpart on the men's side—Ben Hogan.[2]

In addition, Babe was making money by endorsing products—sports equipment, watches, cigarettes. (At that time, people were unaware of the harmful effects of smoking cigarettes. Many athletes endorsed various kinds of tobacco products.) She even signed a contract to put her name on a line of designer women's clothes.[3] Babe was involved in so many money-making activities *Time Magazine* called her "Big Business Babe."[4]

But hitting that little white ball was still Babe's main interest. With 17 consecutive wins behind her, the press and public were anxious to see if she could extend the streak to 18. Now playing as a pro, she made it to the final round against Betty Mims White. Babe was trailing by three holes with three to play. She'd have to win the last three holes to tie and force a playoff. Babe won 16 and 17. Some fans wondered if the pressure was getting to Betty. On the 18th hole Babe sank a birdie. Betty still had to putt. If she too made the putt for a birdie, she and Babe would tie for the hole. That meant Babe would still be one behind. Betty would be the winner.

Betty looked over her putt and then stroked her ball. Plop! She made the putt and won the match by one hole.

Stroke by stroke, Babe extends her winning streak to 17.

Woman of the Year

It could not have been any closer. Betty ended Babe's string at 17.[5]

But in her very next tournament, Babe began another string. Not only did she win the match. She also set an all-time record in the Hard Scrabble Women's Tournament in Little Rock, Arkansas. Babe's score for the tournament was 293. She averaged 73 per round.

Once again, in 1947, Babe was named Woman Athlete of the Year by the Associated Press. In that same year, she received an even greater honor. The Associated Press named Babe Woman of the Year. That award goes beyond sports.[6] It usually goes to leaders in politics, science, medicine, or the arts. The award recognized Babe's impact on people across the country and in other countries. The way she won over the people of Scotland and England, no doubt, had much to do with Babe's receiving this prestigious award. More than being a great athlete, Babe was being recognized as a great human being. That brash and bold girl who was often the outcast was now known throughout the world as Woman of the Year and a role model to all women.

Though Babe was making a fine living through her endorsements and exhibitions, she wasn't making much at tournament golf. There were very few tournaments at which women golfers could earn money. Babe had other sources of income but most of the other pro women golfers did not. So Babe brought a group of these women together and suggested they start a Ladies Professional Golf Association. The others, some of whom had been her

Babe poses for a shot with Jim Thorpe; the two were named top male and female athletes of the first half of the century by the Associated Press.

strongest competitors over the years, agreed.

The LPGA started slowly. While Babe was a national hero, not too many people had much interest in watching other women golfers. In 1949, the LPGA ran nine tournaments offering $15,000 in prizes. But Babe was not discouraged. She worked hard to promote this fledgling organization. Her work paid off. Five years later, the ladies played for $225,000 in prizes.[7] The LPGA continued to grow. Some 54 years later, the LPGA sponsored 33 events across the United States offering prizes totaling more than $42 million. Women from many different countries participated. In 2003, Annika Sorenstam topped the winners list, earning $2 million. In that year, 30 golfers won more than $400,000 each. That was possible only because Babe had paved the way.

In addition, the LPGA provides scholarships to girls and contributes to charities. One of its largest charities is the Susan G. Komen Breast Cancer Foundation.[8] And all of this began because one person, Babe, had the courage and foresight and drive to create something for women.

Patty Berg was one of the original members of the LPGA. She played against Babe many times. She said this about Babe:

> She brought all that humor and showmanship to the game. She humanized it. She was the happiest girl you ever saw, like a kid. Our sport grew because she had so much flair and color. She and I were in competition with each other but she was a great friend of mine. With Babe there was never a dull moment.[9]

To keep things interesting, Fred Corcoran arranged a number of special matches for Babe. In one of these, he proposed that Babe and five other women golfers play against any six male golfers in England. The British took up the offer and brought together the Walker Team. This was a team of Britain's top amateur players. Of course, these men saw little threat in losing to the women.

One of the men, Leonard Crawley, condescendingly said: "I want to play that Babe person." On the first tee,

Mildred "Babe" Didrikson Zaharias

Babe's victories always made for a good story.

Crawley told Babe to go ahead to the ladies' tee. Babe said, "No, I'll shoot from here" (the men's tee). "Then if I beat you," she added, "you'll shave your mustache." The press heard this exchange, and the course was buzzing with the news of Babe's bold challenge. She shot a 74, beating Crawley soundly. For days, the press ragged him about shaving off his mustache.[10] As she so often did, Babe delivered on her boast.

♦♦♦

10
Babe Faces Up To Her Final Challenge

Life was going great for Babe. She was winning tournaments and winning over new friends and fans every day. Then in 1952, things changed once again. While playing in a tournament, she felt a sharp pain. Doctors examined her and located the source of her pain in the thighbone. "Femoral hernia" was the term doctors used. In a short time, though, Babe was back on the golf course. Somewhat weakened, she played in the tournament that was named after her—the Beaumont Babe Zaharias Open. She won the tournament but nearly collapsed. She was rushed to a hospital and was diagnosed with colon cancer.[1]

Babe was down but not out. She agreed to a colostomy, to have the cancerous tissue removed. The sports world

In 1952, Babe won her namesake tournament: the Beaumont Babe Zaharias Open.

Babe makes an amazing come-back.

was saddened. People thought they'd never see Babe play again. But 14 weeks after her surgery, Babe played in the Tam O'Shanter tournament in Chicago. It became clear, however, that she was not strong. In the third round, she took three strokes to make a four-foot putt. Walking to the next tee, she broke down and sobbed. Her dear friend, Betty Dodd, told her to quit, but Babe wouldn't. She got up and finished the round. Then the next day she went out and completed the final round. Later in the year she played in the World Golf Championship and finished third.[2]

People were no longer looking for Babe to win. They were amazed that she would be on the golf course at all. But Babe did win. In 1954, she won five tournaments, including the U.S. Women's Open in Peabody, Massachusetts. She scored a record low 291, beating the runner-up by 12 strokes. Once again, for the sixth time, the

Associated Press named Babe Woman Athlete of the Year. She also won the Ben Hogan Comeback of the Year award. [3]

Why did Babe put herself through so much when she was so weakened by her cancer? Why didn't she just retire and try to enjoy as much of life as she could? She explained that in her autobiography:

> There are several reasons I didn't retire from golf after my cancer surgery in 1953. Every time I get out in a tourney and play well, it seems to buck up people with the same cancer trouble I had. I can tell that from the letters I get. Another is that I helped start the LPGA and I want to keep it growing. At first there were just six or seven of us. Now we've got 25-30 who are very fine golfers. I know the tournaments draw better when all of us are there than just some of us. Since my medical problems, every time I lose two or three in a row, people ask if Babe is through. I have the competitive desire to get back to where I don't want to get beat. I get that old desire to win. And prove all over again that I'm a championship golfer.[4]

Rather than go into seclusion, Babe stayed in the public eye. Even when she could no longer play golf, she showed the feistiness that made her the one and only Babe. She spoke to the press and to the film and television cameras about cancer. She was determined to devote what life she had left to the job of "leading people out of the dark ignorance of cancer." She helped people understand what cancer is, long before we knew what we know today. And she encouraged people to get frequent checkups. "In the name of heaven," she said, "and your own most precious life, never hesitate about the inconvenience or even the cost of a regular physical checkup. Today, if possible.

Outstanding athlete Babe Didrikson celebrates victory with her fans.

Tomorrow is too late."[5]

Mildred "Babe" Didrikson Zaharias died on September 27, 1956. She was 45 years old. Not long after, Ben Hogan and Sam Snead were playing in the Canada Cup tourney. At one point they stopped play and asked for a moment of silence in honor of Babe. In a tournament in Detroit, women players stood around the 18th green. Betty Dodd, Babe's best friend, brought out a guitar and played, because Babe enjoyed music so much. Someone suggested taking up a collection for cancer research. On that one afternoon, they collected $5000.[6] Babe would have been happy knowing she was remembered in a setting she loved so much—a golf course.

It was a fitting tribute to this woman pioneer. She blazed the trail not only for women's golf. Her accomplishments and colorful personality helped change the country's attitude toward all of women's sports.

◆◆◆

Babe's Record of Achievement

- Named All-America in basketball three times.
- Won two gold medals and one silver for track and field in 1932 Olympics.
- Named Woman Athlete of the Year by Associated Press six times (1931, 1945, 1946, 1947, 1950, 1954). No other athlete, man or woman, has received this honor as many times as Babe did.
- Won every major golf championship at least once.
- The first American to win the British Women's Amateur and the first performer to win both the British and United States Women's Amateur tournaments.
- Voted World's Greatest Woman Athlete of the first half of the 20th century by Associated Press.
- Founded Ladies Professional Golf Association.
- Named to the Ladies Golf Hall of Fame.
- Voted number 10 athlete of the 20th Century, the top woman.

Visit the Babe Didrikson Zaharias Museum

You can learn more about Babe and see pictures and film of her at the Babe Didrikson Zaharias museum in Beaumont, Texas. The museum is managed by the Babe Didrikson Zaharias Foundation. In addition to housing the Babe collection, the foundation sponsors various activities to benefit those in need. The foundation also raises funds for scholarships for young girls.

For more information, contact:
Babe Didrikson Zaharias Foundation
P.O. Box 1310
Beaumont, TX 77704
409-838-6681

References

Anderson, Dave. "The Babe Returned from Cancer." May 20, 2004.

Augarde, Tony, ed. *The Oxford Dictionary of Modern Quotations*. New York: Oxford Press, 1991.

The "Babe." Babe Didrikson Zaharias Foundation, Inc. Beaumont, Texas.

Cayleff, Susan E. *Babe Didrikson: The Greatest All-Sport Athlete of All Time*. Berkeley, CA. Conari Press, 1995.

Johnson, William Oscar and Nancy P. Williamson. *Whatta-Gal: The Babe Didrikson Story*. Boston. A Sports Illustrated Book, Little, Brown, and Company. 1975.

LPGA.com.

Schwartz, Larry. "Didrikson was a woman ahead of her time," Special to ESPN.com, June 7, 2004.

Zaharias, Babe Didrikson, as told to Harry Paxton. *This Life I've Led: My Autobiography*. New York: A.S. Barnes and Company, 1955.

About the author...

Cos Ferrara has been a writer for 25 years. A former teacher, he has written for students as well as adults. He brings to the Girls Explore books his experience as a father of three and grandfather of five. His message to our readers is: "The world is large and full of wonder and opportunity. Go out and explore it."

Endnotes

Introduction
1 Dave Anderson. "The Babe Returned from Cancer." May 20, 2004.

Chapter 1–Growing Up Poor But Happy
1 Anderson.

2 William Oscar Johnson and Nancy P. Williamson. *Whatta-Gal: The Babe Didrikson Story*. Boston. A Sports Illustrated Book, Little, Brown, and Company. 1975, p. 37.

3 Susan E. Cayleff. Babe Didrikson: *The Greatest All-Sport Athlete of All Time*. Berkeley, CA. Conari Press, 1995, p. 10.

4 Cayleff, p. 11.

5 Johnson and Williamson, p. 39.

6 Johnson and Williamson, p. 40.

7 Johnson and Williamson, p. 41.

8 Cayleff, p. 8.

9 Cayleff, p. 41.

10 Johnson and Williamson, p. 48.

11 Babe Didrikson Zaharias, as told to Harry Paxton. *This Life I've Led: My Autobiography*. New York: A.S. Barnes and Company, 1955, p. 7.

12 Zaharias, p. 8.

13 Zaharias, p. 7.

14 Cayleff, p. 19.

15 Zaharias, p. 23.

16 Cayleff, p. 28

17 Johnson and Williamson, p. 45.

18 Cayleff, p. 27.

19 Zaharias, p. 29.

20 Zaharias, p. 31.

21 Cayleff, p. 20.
22 Zaharias, p. 27.

Chapter 2–Outcast and Hero
1 Zaharias, p. 33.
2 Cayleff, p. 37.
3 Zaharias, p. 34.
4 Cayleff, p. 38.
5 Johnson and Williamson, p. 55.
6 Johnson and Williamson, p. 55.
7 Johnson and Williamson, p. 54.
8 Cayleff, pp. 36-38.

Chapter 3–Babe Makes Her Move
1 Cayleff, pp. 39-43.
2 Cayleff, pp. 43-45.
3 Johnson and Williamson, p. 64.
4 Zaharias, p. 37.
5 Johnson and Williamson, pp. 62-64.
6 Cayleff, p. 49.
7 Johnson and Williamson, p. 67.
8 Johnson and Williamson, p. 64.
9 Johnson and Williamson, p. 64.
10 Johnson and Williamson, p. 68.
11 Cayleff, pp. 51-52.
12 Zaharias, p. 40.
13 Cayleff, pp. 53-54.
14 Zaharias, p. 41.
15 Zaharias, p. 47.
16 Cayleff, p. 58.
17 Johnson and Williamson, p. 81.
18 Zaharias, p. 48.

19 Zaharias, p. 49.
20 Cayleff, p. 161.
21 Zaharias, p. 50.
22 Johnson and Williamson, pp. 82-83.
23 Cayleff, p. 59.
24 Zaharias, p. 48.

Chapter–Olympic Hero

1 Cayleff, pp. 59-61.
2 Johnson and Williamson, pp. 94-101.
3 Zaharias, p. 53.
4 Zaharias, p. 53.
5 Zaharias, p. 51.
6 Zaharias, p. 55.
7 Zaharias, p. 55.
8 Zaharias, p. 55.
9 Cayleff, p. 65.
10 Zaharias, pp. 56-57.
11 The "Babe." Babe Didrikson Zaharias Foundation, Inc. Beaumont, Texas.
12 Cayleff, p. 69.
13 Cayleff, p. 70.
14 Tony Augarde, ed. The Oxford Dictionary of Modern Quotations. New York: Oxford Press, 1991, p. 180.
15 Cayleff, p. 68.
16 Johnson, p. 107.
17 Cayleff, p. 72.
18 Johnson, p. 110.
19 Johnson, p. 111.

Chapter 5–Babe's Fall from Grace

1 Anderson.
2 Cayleff, pp. 84-85.
3 Johnson, p. 120.

4 Cayleff, p. 90.
5 Johnson, pp. 114-115.
6 Cayleff, p. 89.
7 Schwartz, p. 2.
8 Johnson, pp. 131-133.
9 Cayleff, p. 81.
10 Cayleff, p. 79.
11 Cayleff, p. 81.

Chapter 6–Babe Climbs Back to the Top
1 Johnson, p. 134.
2 Johnson, p. 136.
3 Johnson, p. 137.
4 Johnson, p. 139.
5 Zaharias, p. 87.
6 Cayleff, p. 99.
7 Cayleff, p. 99.
8 Johnson, p. 141.
9 Johnson, p. 149.
10 Cayleff, p. 101.
11 Zaharias, pp. 88-90.
12 Johnson, pp. 141-142.
13 Johnson, p. 142.
14 Cayleff, p. 102.
15 Zaharias, p. 96.
16 Johnson, pp. 145-146.
17 Zaharias, p. 98.
18 Johnson, p. 147.
19 Cayleff, p. 103.
20 Johnson, p. 147.
21 Johnson, p. 154.

Chapter 7–Babe Marries George Zaharias

1 Johnson, p. 156.
2 Johnson, p. 164.
3 Johnson, p. 168.
4 Johnson, p. 169.
5 Johnson, p. 170.
6 Johnson, p. 172.
7 Johnson, pp. 172-174.

Chapter 8–Babe Hits Her Stride

1 Johnson, p. 175.
2 Johnson, p. 175.
3 Cayleff, p. 126.
4 Johnson, p. 176.
5 Cayleff, pp. 128-129.
6 Johnson, p. 178-9.
7 Johnson, p. 179.
8 Johnson, p. 181.
9 Johnson, pp. 181-182.

Chapter 9– Woman of the Year

1 Johnson, p. 182.
2 Cayleff, p. 135.
3 Cayleff, p. 131.
4 Cayleff, p. 135.
5 Johnson, p. 184.
6 Cayleff, p. 131.
7 Johnson, pp. 190-191.
8 LPGA.com.
9 Johnson, p. 190.
10 Johnson, p. 194.

Chapter 10–Babe Faces Up to Her Final Challege

1 Cayleff, p. 131.
2 Johnson, p. 210.
3 Johnson, p. 210.
4 Zaharias, pp. 228-29.
5 Anderson.
6 Johnson, p. 217.